The Blended Learning Cookbook

by Clive Shepherd

Published in collaboration with Saffron Interactive

First published in the United Kingdom in 2005.

ISBN: 0-9545904-8-1

Layout Production – Jenni Grove, Saffron Interactive

Cover Art Design – Jenni Grove, Saffron Interactive

Contents

Preface

Some would argue that, like pills that promise weight loss while you sleep, e-learning has promised much and delivered little. And now, we have a new pill in the guise of blended learning and we are all left wondering if this pill, which looks and feels different, will provide us with similar results. In order to provide some clarity to the situation, we asked Clive Sheppard to put together this cookbook. A book that will provide practitioners with examples of outstanding successes and blueprints for best practice. This cookbook is for anyone who wishes to improve the effectiveness of their current training interventions, who wants to understand how e-learning can be integrated into a broader learning process and for anyone looking for innovative approaches to training.

Hanif Sazen

Hanif Sazen is Chief Executive Officer of Saffron Interactive, a business communications company providing blended learning solutions to organisations in the Global 500.

SAFFRON
INTERACTIVE

Northburgh House
10 Northburgh Street
London
EC1V 0AT

Tel: 0207 490 9930
Fax: 0207 253 5248
info@saffroninteractive.com
www.saffroninteractive.com

Blended learning is the thing

Blended learning is the thing. Training's big talking point for the mid noughties. Like sensitivity training, action learning, interactive video, accelerated learning, coaching and mentoring, and e-learning before it, it has become a bit of a bandwagon. As a result, no self-respecting member of the training cognoscenti (yes, they like to think that's what they are) will treat it with anything other than scorn and cynicism; another panacea to delude the masses, to fade into the background like its predecessors when we eventually realise it doesn't work. I once went to a seminar where the chairperson referred to it as the 'b' word, something not to be mentioned in polite company. I am not so shy about the subject – blended learning (there, I said it) is more than just a fad, it's a recognition that other training methods out there are simply not strong enough to work for all audiences, all of the time. Sometimes, only a combination of learning methods will do the job.

Handling objections

One of the most common objections to the razzmatazz about blended learning is that it's nothing new – blending is something we have always done. There is obviously some truth in this, because we can probably all think of some examples of training interventions that have successfully combined a variety of media. But to maintain that this has been in any way the norm is clearly wide of the mark. Most learning, of course, is informal – we don't even know that it is happening. When it is structured and formalised, it's most likely to be wholly on-job, if not wholly in the classroom, if not wholly online. Blending has been (and still is) very much the exception, not the rule. That's not surprising because blending is a hassle, it takes more planning and more co-ordination.

Cynics may also claim that blended learning is just a rebranding exercise, carried out by e-learning vendors who have hit upon hard times after the bursting of the dotcom bubble. Again, there is something to be said for this view. Most companies who claim to be in the blended learning business used to be – you guessed it – e-learning companies, not classroom trainers. They even tried to make the term blended learning their own, referring to it as a mix of 'e-learning and traditional methods'. This definition still dominates, even though it is unhelpfully restrictive, not to say condescending about the so-called 'traditional' methods.

The e-learning community may retaliate by claiming that blended learning is in fact a sop to the classroom community, allowing them a piece of the action in a world of learning that will be increasingly dominated by the computer. This view is hard to justify. Computers are playing an increasing role in learning, but have major limitations, as we shall see. Even the most optimistic forecasts for e-learning don't see it overtaking the classroom as a training method.

Others object to blended learning not for what it means in theory but for how it is often applied in practice, i.e. use the classroom for anything that involves people and computers for the boring stuff. In his book Lessons in Learning, e-Learning and Training, Roger Schank laments that "the part that is assigned to e-learning is the rote learning part – the facts followed by the answers. That stuff doesn't stick, and for the most part trainees hate it. When you hear the word 'blended', run." Now Roger may be right – he often is – but for me what he says is really an argument for blending more effectively; being a brighter blender. Very much the point of this book.

Coming to terms with blended learning

A few years ago, I thought I had a pretty good understanding of what blended learning was about – you know, combining online and traditional elements to build courses that used the best of the old and the new. That is, until I sat at breakfast watching my wife open her Open University package – then I realised that not only was I unduly restrictive in my definition of what blended learning meant, but that when it came to imaginative combinations of ingredients, I was a complete amateur. Out of the box came workbooks, good old-fashioned text books, cassettes containing interviews, lectures and extracts from pieces of music, and books full of nothing but full-colour pictures. Then there were the TV programmes that were aired in the middle of the night for you to record and watch later, phone tutorials with your personal tutor, occasional group sessions with local members of your course and, to top it all, the one-week summer school. In this instance there wasn't a single online element (although subsequently, discussion forums have been added), but I defy anyone to say that this wasn't a first class example of blended learning: a broad range of media was used to present information, there were numerous self-study activities, opportunities to seek expert advice and a chance to collaborate with fellow learners (in the case of the latter, probably not enough to satisfy most learners, but a reasonable attempt given the budget). Well done the OU.

In coming to terms with blended learning, it's helpful to start with what it is not. First of all, it is not providing learners with choices of how to undergo a piece of training – you can have e-learning or, if you prefer, the classroom. Not only are learners failing to get a blended solution (which means they get all the disadvantages of a single method, as well as the advantages, whereas a blend can smooth out the rough edges), but you're having to pay to implement two solutions instead of one. A blended solution is also not a way of combining a number of very similar elements, say books, videos and CD-ROMs. The learner gets some variety in their self-study, but self-study is as far as it goes. A successful blended solution is like a balanced meal, combining a range of ingredients, each of which has a unique purpose.

I would define blended learning as an approach to the design of learning interventions which mixes learning media appropriately, to achieve solutions which are both effective and efficient. It's easy to create blends that are effective, if you throw enough resources at the job. Similarly, it's easy to be efficient and conserve resources, if you let quality go down the pan. The challenge for the designer is to create solutions that are both effective and practical, given the inevitable resource limitations that we all work under.

Blended learning also takes account of differences in learning objectives, the characteristics and preferences of learners and the practicalities of the particular situation. If you're not sensitive to these differences, the chances are you'll come up with the same familiar solution all the time, one with which you are comfortable but that doesn't necessarily deliver for learners. A good example is the classic 'classroom sandwich', in which a classroom course is topped and tailed with a little e-learning. This may be the right method in some situations; in others it could just be going through the motions.

Creating the right blends is a tough task for the 21st century trainer, because as soon as we started networking computers together we created a whole range of new options (online self-study, virtual classrooms, discussion forums, chat rooms and email support, not to mention podcasts and other mobile solutions), each of which has to be considered alongside more than a dozen existing options. They have to be considered because they may be more effective or more efficient for your particular mix of learning objectives, target audiences and resource constraints. What we don't need are unnecessary complications like having to include something online in the mix when it isn't needed, or having to include a non-online option when we're getting all we need from our various online options. Not to mention the fact that we don't need a blend at all for the vast majority of short courses. Now there's a thought.

What makes good learning?

To conclude this, merely the first step in our quest for better blends for better learning, I thought it would be useful to establish some measures of success. What exactly is good learning? Would we know it if we saw it? Now we all have our own ideas on this one, but mine are the ones that count here, because these are my fingers on the keyboard.

Effective learning, at least as far as adults are concerned and in the context of their work, more than anything else needs to be relevant. When it's relevant, it matters; it makes a difference to their job performance or to their job prospects. Most open learning materials, made freely available over an organisation's intranet or in an open learning centre, are insufficiently relevant, which is why they are rarely used. Relevance is important, because if you get this right, your learner is likely to be engaged, without a lot of fancy extras.

Relevance can be increased by the way that you design a learning intervention: build on the learner's existing knowledge, use plenty of examples that relate directly to the learner's work experience, make frequent use of stories and anecdotes. All of these techniques are inductive in nature – they move from the specific to the general, from the concrete to the theoretical. Learners like this, because by and large they struggle to find theory relevant.

Adult learners also like to be in control. They like to determine when learning takes place (ideally just before it's needed), where it takes place and how long it lasts. Sometimes small chunks are best, sometimes sustained immersion. Sometimes they like to whip through at speed, sometimes to labour over each point. Being in control also includes the ability to ask questions whenever you want, whether that's of tutors or fellow learners; which is why pure self-study can sometimes be a let down – it denies the learner the fundamental right of questioning.

Finally, when they're at work, adults are more interested in 'knowing how' than 'knowing that'. They want skills that they can employ to their advantage in their jobs, and there's only one way to develop skills. "How do you get to Carnegie Hall?" asked the tourist in New York. "Practise," came the quick-witted response. Most training falls down because it fails to provide adequate opportunities for practice. It spends two days teaching you how to handle customer complaints, then allows you maybe ten minutes to try this out with a colleague. Just long enough, in fact, for you to realise how bad you are. Trainers could learn from tennis coaches. They spend a few minutes demonstrating the correct strokes, then reinforce these over thousands of hours of repetitive practice.

As we shall see in subsequent chapters, almost any training method can contribute something useful in terms of learning effectiveness; equally, every method has inherent weaknesses which are capable of getting in the way. Often, the only way of satisfying every criterion for 'good learning' is to use a bit of this and a bit of that, which is where we came in. Before we explore this possibility in more detail, a word of warning. Getting the right blend is not enough, you also have to design and implement it well. Thomas L. Russell undertook an analysis of more than 350 studies conducted over the past 50 years, each attempting to compare the effectiveness of one learning medium with another. The title of Russell's book is The No Significant Difference Phenomenon, which says it all. His conclusion? It's not what you do, it's the way that you do it.

Testing the case for blended learning

In chapter one, I described what I thought blended learning was all about and attempted to handle some of the more common objections raised by its detractors. I also diverted a little off the path to explore what 'good learning' might actually look like, because only when this is clear in our minds can we judge whether blending learning methods actually help us to achieve this goal.

In chapter two, I attempt an analysis of blended learning's main competitors – the classroom, the computer and on-job instruction, when these are employed as the exclusive vehicles for satisfying learning objectives. As a result, I hope to prove that, however strong these competitors may seem when used for the right purpose, with the right audience and at the right time, each has fatal flaws which render them ineffective or inefficient as universal solutions. The longer, the more ambitious or the more complex a training programme becomes, the stronger the argument for adopting a blended approach. Let's see.

Why classrooms aren't enough

Even with the slow but determined growth of e-learning, the overwhelming majority of all formal, off-job training that is carried out in the workplace takes place in classrooms; this after most students have experienced ten to twenty years of almost entirely classroom-based education. Unless teachers and trainers are all fools, which is unlikely, there must be some pretty good reasons why the classroom is so dominant. Here's a few. First and foremost, the classroom is convenient – it gathers learners together away from distractions (which in the case of adults means their jobs, but for children means opportunities for annoying adults and generally being naughty), under the guidance of a single minder, also known as a teacher, trainer or whatever. Because of the fiddle involved in gathering learners in one place (school runs, train journeys, flights, etc.), classroom sessions are traditionally measured in days rather than hours. The block-booking of learning time helps both parents/managers and learners to plan ahead. It also makes for easy administration for those people who have to book people on courses and track their progress.

The collective nature of classroom learning has other advantages. Purely economically, the bigger the class, the greater the efficiencies over one-to-one learning, albeit at the expense of individual attention. More importantly – and assuming the event doesn't become overly competitive – learners like being with each other. They value the potential for friendship, support and shared experience. The show-offs gain an audience. The meek can sit at the back and avoid eye contact with the trainer.

The strengths of classroom education – learning in groups, away from the work environment, at pre-determined times and for fixed periods – are, of course, also the weaknesses. The problem with groups is that they are actually a collection of individuals, with different work priorities, different starting points in terms of knowledge, skills and attitudes, and different preferences when it comes to how they learn. It is impossible to design a classroom session which, in the amount of time likely to be available, fully satisfies the needs of every participant. This difficulty is most apparent when the objective is to impart knowledge – while one person is struggling to keep up, another is twiddling their thumbs; while one is captivated by a subject that is highly relevant to their work, another is eagerly awaiting a change of topic. This is frustrating for participants; it's also highly inefficient, which is why self-study methods are typically fifty percent faster.

When the objectives become more ambitious than simply imparting knowledge, groups have more to offer. Debate and discussion can help develop understanding and influence attitudes; case studies and other group exercises can foster cognitive skills; role-plays provide an opportunity to practise interpersonal skills. While this interaction can be accomplished online, it is unlikely to be so easy to administer or facilitate. However, it is important to recognise that activities carried out in the classroom are not the real thing. Working with a group on a marketing case study is not the same thing as working alone, late into the night on a real marketing campaign. Role-playing a sales call takes you only so far in preparing you to face a real customer. And many skills simply cannot be simulated in the classroom, because of the physical limitations of the space.

The other difficulty with classroom education relates to the necessity to gather with like-minded learners at the same place and at the same time, for a scheduled event. This requires you to travel to the event, perhaps even to stay overnight. It requires you to wait until the event is next scheduled to run, even though your needs may be urgent. It also requires you to do all your learning in a single block, when this may be more effectively – and sometimes more conveniently – handled in small chunks. And, perhaps most importantly of all, it requires you to make all the running in transferring what you have learned to the work environment. It treats learning as an event, an episode, rather than a natural element of all working life. Events, whether they are classroom courses, concerts, plays, TV programmes or football matches, can change people's lives. More typically they are appreciated at the time, and then filed away and forgotten.

Why computers aren't enough

When any trainer is first introduced to the concept of e-learning, they are likely to come up with the same key questions. What exactly is e-learning, and when should I use it? The first question is harder to answer than it sounds, because you have to explain all the ways that computer networks can facilitate learning, by providing learners with access to materials, to tutors and other learners. The answer to the first question then makes the second that much harder. Each e-learning method has its own unique features and benefits, and hence its own place in the design of online and blended solutions. Nevertheless, if the trainer sticks with it, they will get to see how e-learning in its various forms can make a contribution, particularly in the teaching of knowledge – of facts, concepts, rules, principles, processes and procedures. When it comes to skills, they don't get it.

Skills are important in training because very few of us get paid for what we know; we are employed because of what we can do. It's not enough to know that, we have to know how. If the emphasis in education is 80:20 in favour of knowing that, in training the priorities are reversed. So, good question, can computers really help us to learn skills? The answer, of course, is that it all depends.

Skills are rarely taught in isolation. There's typically a sequence starting with the imparting of some basic supporting information, moving on to some sort of demonstration of the skill, then the practice of that skill by the learner (ideally with objective feedback) and culminating in application of the skill in the real work environment. I don't think anyone would argue that computers can help in the first step, but then that's just a question of knowledge again. They certainly could assist in the second, because almost any skill can be demonstrated using graphics, animation, audio or video, and, thanks to broadband, all of these media are now available to us (imagine using video to demonstrate interpersonal skills such as complaint handling or closing a sale). Computers might also be able to help at stage three, in providing practice with feedback, but here it depends on the type of skill.

Some skills are essentially cognitive, involving problem-solving, planning and decision-making; and in a knowledge society, so much of what we do falls under this category – programming, writing reports, analysing data, planning projects, creating marketing strategies. These jobs are usually carried out on a computer, so it's not too far-fetched to believe that you could practise them in the same way. The issue, of course, is how you get feedback on your code, your reports, your analyses, project plans and strategies. Computer software could be devised to examine your work and give you personalised feedback, but this is likely to be complicated and unreliable. Where computer networks can help, is in allowing you to share your work electronically with tutors and colleagues, wherever they are in the world, and to discuss your work using email, instant messaging and discussion forums.

Let's move on to interpersonal skills, the ones that involve you interacting with customers, suppliers, bosses, peers and subordinates. A fair amount of success can be achieved by designing software that helps you to take your first steps in applying these skills – scenarios that you observe and critique, scenarios in which you are an active participant and determine what happens next. However, these are first steps and not as authentic as the experiences that can be laid on in the classroom, where you have the opportunity to role-play and receive direct feedback from real humans. But even this is not enough. No skills can be learned from one or two practice sessions – the learner needs to continue their development on-the-job, getting feedback on an ongoing basis from their manager or coach.

The third category of skill is the psychomotor: practical skills that involve you interacting with the physical environment – operating machines, driving tanks, lifting parcels or cutting down trees. Classrooms and computers are of little use when it comes to practising many psychomotor skills, although there are exceptions. When the skill is computer-related, such as typing or using a mouse, then it's not surprising to find users learning on the computer itself. More important is the use of simulators to teach those skills which are too costly and too hazardous to learn in the real-world – flying planes, operating nuclear power plants, navigating an oil rig.

So can computers teach skills? Well, as we've seen, they can help in the early stages of learning any skill. When the skills are cognitive, they may be able to do the whole job – less so with interpersonal and psychomotor skills. So, e-learning is no more a panacea than the classroom, which leaves us with good old Nellie.

Why Nellie's not enough

'Sitting next to Nellie', more properly known as on-job instruction, is familiar to us all, as the way we get to learn the details of our jobs when more formal methods are not available, i.e. much of the time. Nellie's been hard at work as a part-time trainer for thousands of years, long before classrooms, books, videos and computers appeared to provide her with some much needed help. Nellie's also capable of being highly effective, providing highly individualised instruction at the point of need, whenever and wherever that may be. Nellie's pupils don't get bored because she concentrates on only the most relevant and practical issues, ignores useless theory, and places the priority on 'you doing' rather than 'her telling'. (This Nellie is, of course, idealised. Some Nellies have been known to be unavailable, unprepared, unresponsive, impatient, rambling and even asleep. Nellies cannot be relied upon totally.)

Personal tuition is nice while it lasts, which usually means as long as you can afford it. Which is why super-rich, top-ten tennis players employ world-class coaches to travel with them on the tour, practise with them every day and generally agonise about ways of achieving one percent improvements in performance; it's also why our kids have their tennis lessons in large groups of mixed ability, get to hit only a few balls a week and more often than not remain in a state of conscious incompetence.

One-to-one tuition is intensive because you, the learner, are always working. All too often, it provides inadequate opportunities for debate, for exploration and for reflection. It rarely comes with top-quality learning materials – videos, trouble-shooting guides, white papers and checklists – which stimulate thought and provide ongoing reference. These opportunities are more likely to be provided in formal, off-job learning situations, employing – you guessed it – classrooms and computers. The fact is we need all these learning methods and more; we simply cannot rely on them to do the whole job in every situation. We blend because we want our learners to achieve the best results possible at every point in their training programme, within a realistic timeframe and at a realistic cost. And that's the challenge.

A logical approach to blended learning

In this third and final introductory chapter, I explore what I believe to be the three most important elements in a systematic approach to the design of effective and efficient blended learning solutions: analysing the unique characteristics of the situation in which the solution is to be deployed; selecting an appropriate training strategy and methods to meet the needs of the situation; and determining the communication media best suited to the chosen strategy. If this sounds abstract and theoretical, stick with me, because the process can be quickly and easily applied in practice.

First take a look at the situation

Chances are that just about every systematic approach to training that you've ever encountered starts with some form of analysis – you know, job analysis, task analysis, needs analysis, that sort of thing. You're sure that some poor trainer out there is actually doing this sort of thing, you're just glad it isn't you. Well, there's some analysis in this model as well and, sorry, it has to be conducted first, before you get onto the more enjoyable, creative bits. The reason why analysis is necessary in the real world, not only in textbooks, is because just about every training situation is different, different enough to demand a different solution. If you treat every situation the same, then you apply the same solution again and again, whether or not it is really suitable. Lazy thinking like this is what leads to catalogues full of training courses all using the same method, such as the classroom. I know this isn't true where you work, but believe me, it happens.

One way in which situations differ is in the nature of the learning that you would like to see happen. We don't need to get into a detailed discussion here of the ways in which learning objectives can be classified, but it's important to understand what a difference these make. If your objectives have a knowledge and understanding component (a need to learn facts, principles, concepts, rules, processes, procedures, etc.), then this will influence your choice of strategy (because some strategies are more successful than others at meeting knowledge and understanding objectives) and your subsequent choice of medium (because some of these are better suited than others to making the strategy work). The same is true with other types of learning objectives (cognitive skills, interpersonal skills, psychomotor skills, attitudes) – each demands a radically different strategy, which in turn dictates the most appropriate communication medium. How different is different? Well, consider an outward bound leadership course in the Lake District, an online, networked marketing business game, a simulator for a military jet, an induction booklet, a negotiation skills workshop. Chances are they are trying to meet some very different objectives, wouldn't you think?

Equally important is the way in which audiences differ from one training situation to another. Of course there are the demographics – age, gender and the suchlike, which might influence your design. Of more significance is likely to be what they already know about the subject in question, what their attitude is to this subject, and what associated skills they currently possess. It matters most when these starting positions vary a great deal from person to person, because this can make it more difficult to work with them in groups (such as in a classroom) and to follow any form of uniform and fixed curriculum. The same problems can be experienced when learners differ substantially in terms of their own objectives (irrespective of what they already know or can do), because of different priorities in their jobs and careers.

Learners also differ in what psychologists like to call their metacognitive skills, their ability to self-direct their own learning. Some learners are more dependent than others on structure in the learning process; some are quite capable of tackling just about any subject on their own. This matters a great deal, because you simply cannot expect those with poor metacognitive skills to flourish in a free-form, exploratory learning environment. Similarly, independent learners can become frustrated by what they see as the stifling formality and rigid structure imposed by many classroom events and interactive e-learning courses.

Learners also differ to some extent in their preferred learning styles, whether you believe these are relatively fixed characteristics, or that they vary depending on what the learner is being asked to learn. There are various ways of modelling these differences (visual, auditory, kinaesthetic; activist, pragmatist, theorist, reflector et al), each with their own tests and instruments to help learners diagnose their particular preferences. What's clear, though, is that learners are quite capable of learning in any number of ways, whether or not they prefer the method that's been selected for them. It's also clear that, unless you're sure that the majority of your audience have roughly the same preferences (it doesn't take a genius to know that you'll need to design a different course for accountants than for salespeople), there's not a lot you can do about it except to build as much variety into your course as you can; an argument for blending, perhaps?

There is one more way in which situations vary and this is in terms of the simple practicalities. Practicalities are important because training solutions have to be efficient as well as effective – working within available timescales and budgets. A number of factors influence timescales and budgets, including the geographical location of learners (because travel and subsistence are often the largest costs you'll have), the availability of facilities and equipment (because if you don't have them you'll have to buy or rent them), and the skills at your disposal in-house (because if you don't have the project managers, the designers, the trainers, the tutors and others that you need, you'll have to resource these externally, which takes time and costs more than working with what you've got).

Then you establish a method

Once you have a firm grasp of the situation – the type of learning required, the nature of your target audience and the practical constraints – you can begin to design an appropriate solution, starting with an appropriate overall strategy. Clark and Wittrock (2001) have a useful model for analysing strategies according to the degree of control imposed over the process by the trainer and/or the student. At the most trainer-centred end of the spectrum is simple exposition – the trainer tells the learner things, using methods such as lectures and prescribed reading; no interaction is expected or required, except perhaps some Q&A or an assessment.

The second strategy – structured instruction – is still under the trainer's overall control, but is much more interactive, allowing the trainer to fine-tune the process to the needs of the particular audience. Structured instruction is widely used in training, and includes most classroom sessions, most computer-based self-study materials and much formal on-job instruction. Dependent learners rely on this degree of structure; independent learners (which include many of those who have passed through higher education, as well as those used to taking advantage of the wider availability of knowledge through the Internet) can do without.

A more learner-centred strategy is guided discovery, in which learners engage in tasks that have been specially designed to provide them with opportunities for experimentation with alternative approaches. Learners improve their skill or understanding by reflecting, with the help of facilitators, coaches or mentors, upon the outcomes of these tasks and, as a result, drawing general conclusions which they can apply to future tasks. Guided discovery is experiential; it allows learners to have a go and learn from their mistakes. This strategy can be deployed in face-to-face settings, whether one-to-one, outdoors (as in Outward Bound courses) or in the classroom; through computer-based case studies, games and simulations; or through project work.

The final strategy is exploration – each learner determines their own learning process, taking advantage of resources provided by trainers and others, and takes out of this process their own, unique learning. Exploration may seem a relatively informal strategy, but no less useful for that. In fact it's probably the way that most learning takes place.

The learning process underlying any of these top-level strategies is likely to have a number of key stages or elements, for example: preparing the learner, presenting learning content, providing opportunities for practice, offering feedback, providing opportunities for reflection and planning, application to the real-job environment, providing ongoing support. The exact nature of these stages or elements will depend on your objectives and your chosen strategy. The important issue here is that you attempt to separate out those aspects of the learning process that are very different in character, because there is a good chance that you'll benefit from applying different methods and different media to the different elements. This is where the opportunities arise for blended learning. If you can't sensibly break down the process for your given situation, that's not a problem – you can probably save yourself some trouble and use a single medium.

Only now do you select the medium

You'll want to flesh out your strategy by selecting specific methods for use at each stage. There are hundreds to choose from, a selection of which is listed in appendix 3. Note that very few of these methods are tied to a specific learning medium – they can usually be applied in more than one way, perhaps online, face-to-face, even over the phone. It's an important aspect of this approach to blended learning that you leave the choice of medium until last. First you establish the methods that you believe will be effective in meeting the demands of your particular session. You then select the most appropriate medium for each of these methods, looking to optimise efficiency without compromising on effectiveness. If you choose more than one medium, you have a blend. If the same medium works in each case, you do not.

Technology has increased the selection of media available to teachers and trainers. Of course all learning was originally conducted face-to-face, providing an immediacy to the interaction, a rich sensory experience (you see, you hear, you touch, you smell) and, if you're lucky enough to be one-on-one, the ultimate in personalisation. Books, when they arrived, provided the counterbalance, by allowing learners more independence and the ability to control the pace. The invention of the telephone provided additional connectivity for learners and tutors working at a distance. Videos, CDs and all their variants added to the diversity of offline media and made high-quality audio and video available to distance learners. But perhaps the most significant new medium made available by technology is the networked computer, connecting learners to as many as a billion other Internet users and countless billions of web pages. E-learning is the rather inadequate name we give to the use of networked computers as a medium to facilitate learning. It is not a single method – like the face-to-face channel, it is capable of supporting a wide variety of methods, many of which have almost certainly not yet been invented.

A little pragmatism

Systematic approaches are rarely followed to the letter in the real world – after all, let's face it, life's just too short. What's important is that when we cut corners, we do so consciously, applying the main principles with common sense and a great deal of pragmatism. The rest of this book is laden with examples of typical training situations and uncomplicated blended solutions. If you find it hard (or simply too boring) to apply the systematic approach, you're welcome to copy any of the examples which you find relevant to your experience. The end result should be the same – more effective, efficient training solutions.

Recipe 1: Product updates

The situation

The organisation is a large multinational electronics company, with a catalogue of thousands of products. New products are launched practically every week, typically offering minor variants and improvements on existing products.

The organisation needs to keep its international sales force and team of engineers conversant with the new products. This requires that they know the major discriminating characteristics of each new product, the benefits that these afford the customer, and the implications these have for technical support and maintenance.

The audience for the training consists of technically competent and experienced professionals, who already have a good understanding of the organisation's product line. They are widely distributed geographically, working from country offices or from their homes, but have easy broadband access to the organisation's intranet. Their busy schedule of appointments allows them only a minimal time to spend on product training.

The training for each new product must be prepared and delivered prior to launch, a lead time of a couple of weeks at best. With their other responsibilities, product managers and technical trainers have little time to devote to new product training.

The strategy

The organisation has chosen to use an exposition strategy. They believe that the target audience are sufficiently independent learners and have sufficient experience to benefit from this approach. It also allows them to prepare and deliver the training in a minimum of time.

The blend

Elements	Methods	Media
Preparation.	Announce the training.	Email / SMS messaging.
Delivery.	Presentation. Subject matter support (Q&A). Viewing recorded video material.	Virtual Classroom. Virtual Classroom. Recording of virtual. classroom session (for those that miss the live session).
Application.	Performance support / reference.	Web pages on intranet. Downloadable PDF documents.

The rationale

The organisation has chosen to use online media exclusively to fulfil this strategy, an obvious choice given the wide geographic distribution of the audience, time constraints and ready availability of technology. The primary delivery mechanism is a virtual classroom, providing the ability for the trainer to speak to the audience live with audio, to show slides and handle any questions. The session could be run more than once to accommodate different time zones.

The performance support materials provide easy ongoing reference at a much greater level of detail, making use of existing marketing and technical reference materials.

Recipe 2: Detailed policies and procedures

The situation

The organisation is the credit card division of a major bank. The bank is re-organising its call centres so that all operators will be capable of handling all types of calls, whereas in the past different departments had specialised in particular aspects of the customer relationship (new accounts, customer service, credit and collection, etc.).

The learning consists almost entirely of rules and procedures. The sum total of these is considerable, although all learners will have had experience of a sizeable slice (perhaps 25%). Some of the rules and procedures apply generally across many circumstances. Others are likely to be applied only in exceptional circumstances.

Two thousand learners need to be trained. Although they have experience of the subject matter, they are not typically independent learners and will benefit from a structured approach. More than half of the audience could be categorised as activists, enjoying practical activity and interaction with their peers.

Operators are split evenly between three major centres around the UK, each with its own classroom training facilities. The training department has four months in which to design and implement the solution, with should have the minimum possible impact on the ongoing business. The department has plenty of skilled and qualified trainers for whom this training is their main priority. They also have funds to engage outside suppliers if necessary.

The strategy

The organisation has chosen to use a structured instruction strategy, based on the nature of the learning required and the characteristics of the target audience. The group sessions also incorporate an element of guided discovery using case studies, scenarios and group discussion.

The blend

Elements	Methods	Media
Preparation.	Reading (about the training and how it will be organised).	Web pages on intranet.
Delivery (to address only the most general rules and procedures).	Group instruction. Group activities/exercises (case studies and scenarios). Facitilated group discussion. Group progress review.	Classroom. Classroom. Classroom. Classroom.
Application (to address less commonly applied rules and procedures).	Performance support / reference.	Web page on intranet.

The rationale

The most important feature of this approach is the decision to restrict the formal delivery element to the most general rules and procedures. This shortens the training considerably and avoids the danger of overload. It also makes time available for the more important rules to be properly explored and discussed. The classroom was chosen because of the availability of trainers and classroom facilities, the fact that learners would not have to travel to the sessions, the fact that training could be accomplished in a single session, and the suitability of the setting for group work and discussion.

The intranet was chosen for the reference material because of its availability to every learner at their desktop, the speed with which information could be accessed and the ease with which material could be maintained.

Recipe 3: In-company MBA course

The situation

The organisation is a large multinational company with regional headquarters in Brussels, Singapore and Dallas. They are organising an in-house, two-year Master of Business Administration course for 24 middle-managers, split evenly across the three regional offices.

The learning will be academic in nature, made more relevant, where possible, by practical work centring on issues faced by individual participants and the company as a whole. Expected learning outcomes include a broad knowledge and understanding of business issues, as well as advanced problem-solving skills.

Learners are aged between 28 and 45, mostly graduates, with several years' management experience and an ability to learn independently where required. All are fluent in English as a first or second language.

The distance between the regional centres is a major practical constraint.

The strategy

The faculty has decided to adopt a mixed approach of simple exposition, for delivery of the core curriculum, guided discovery as a way of building understanding and problem-solving skills, with an element of exploration in the work towards the assignments.

The blend

Elements	Methods	Media
Preparation.	Reading (about the course).	Web pages within the Virtual Learning Environment (VLE). Online (accessed from the VLE)
	Individual questionnaire (to assess prior knowledge, personal goals, learning preferences, potential problems, etc.).	
	Syndicate group presentation and facilitated discussion. Ice-breaking activity (whole group). One-to-one coaching/support.	Face-to-face small group meeting (tutor travels to the home country of the syndicate group). Bulletin board (part of VLE). Email. Telephone.
Delivery to core curriculum (interspersed with practicle work below).	Lectures. Prescribed reading. One-to-one subject matter support.	Virtual Classroom. Books. Email. Telephone.
Practicle work.	Syndicate group activites (case studies, scenarios).	Participants communicate locally face-to-face, by email and telephone; results using the bulletin board
	Inter-syndicate group business game.	Game is run online; communication as above.
	Syndicate group assignments. Unfacilitated sysndicate group discussion (for planning / reflection). Facilitated group discussion.	Communication as above. Face-to-face (locally). Bulletin board.
Assessment.	Individual project / assignment.	Individual work (no medium required).
	One-to-one progress review.	Email. Telephone.
Review.	Group progress review.	Bulletin board.

The rationale

Because of the distance problem, the organisation has opted for online communication within the group as a whole as well as for lectures (using a virtual classroom). Care will have to be taken in scheduling these live events to take consideration of time zone differences, although they can be recorded for those not able to attend at the scheduled time. The majority of communication is asynchronous, using bulletin boards, email and web documents.

Syndicate groups are able to work together locally, including face-to-face sessions where required. Note how the tutor travels to meet with the syndicate groups at the start of the programme.

Recipe 4: Telephone customer service

The situation

The organisation is a government department that is soon to launch a new help line for businesses. To provide this service they have employed 200 new staff to work in a brand new call centre. They have already provided the staff with an induction to the organisation and training is in progress to familiarise staff with the information they will be expected to supply to callers. To ensure a consistently high level of customer service, the organisation now requires all staff to receive telephone customer service training.

The primary learning objective is to develop interpersonal skills, although there is an attitudinal component as well.

The audience varies in the amount of telephone customer service experience they possess. The majority are not used to learning independently.

There are few practical constraints as all staff are working in the same centre, which has excellent training facilities, including computer classrooms. However, a shortage of time means that not everyone will be able to receive group training before the help line opens.

The strategy

The training department has decided to adopt a structured instruction strategy, believing that the audience will respond better to a structured approach and that the strategy is well suited to the training of interpersonal skills.

The blend

Elements	Methods	Media
Preparation.	Group presentations (to provide an overview of the training programme and handle queries).	Classroom.

Preliminary training.	Interactive self-study lessons.	Online over the intranet (using customised off-the-shelf materials).
	Individual activities and excersises (including case studies and scenarios).	Online over the intranet (using customised off-the-shelf materials).
	One-to-one progress review.	Face-to-face.
Primary skills training.	Group ice-breaking activity.	Classroom.
	Group instruction.	Classroom.
	Facilitated group discussion.	Classroom.
	Individual practice (observed by the trainer and the learners).	Classroom.
	Group progress review.	Classroom.
Ongoing skill development.	One-to-one coaching.	Face-to-face.

The rationale

An important decision has been made to provide preliminary training on a self-study basis (although they could also allow this training to take place at the computer in twos or threes). This solves two problems: first, the variability in learners' customer service experience; and second, the need for some foundation knowledge and skills to be imparted before learners get the opportunity to attend the classroom sessions. The face-to-face progress reviews ensure learners are able to resolve any difficulties they are experiencing with the self-study materials.

The classroom has been selected for the primary skills training, as this provides a better environment for skills practice, using role play exercises, and discussion of customer service issues. Because all learners will have completed the preliminary training, all members of the classroom group will have the same foundation knowledge and skills.

Because continued practice and feedback is essential to achieving the learning objectives, ongoing coaching is provided face-to-face in the workplace.

Recipe 5: Company induction

The situation

The organisation is a fast-growing UK retail fashion chain appealing primarily to a young audience and with a reputation for 'attitude'. The company's offices and warehouses are based at one location in the Midlands. They are looking to set up a new company induction programme to be taken by all new full-time staff before they join their branches or departments.

The company wants to use the company induction to familiarise new starters with the company's history, culture and business values. It would also like new starters to be aware of the basic mechanics of the business and the critical factors driving its success in a highly-competitive market. More detailed training in company policies will follow.

The majority of new starters are outgoing young people with an interest in fashion and a modern lifestyle. They are likely to be tech-savvy. Many of them will have had no previous retail experience, other than perhaps the odd part-time job. Only a minority will have gone through higher education.

Between 10 and 20 new starters join the company every week, primarily to work in branches around the UK. The company would like the company induction to be brief but high impact.

The strategy

The company has decided to divide the induction into three phases: self-study work carried out by learners individually before joining, a formal induction session on day one, and a resource for ongoing reference. To make the self-study as interesting and challenging as possible, they have adopted a guided discovery strategy, using games and quizzes to stimulate learners to find out information about the company from the textual, graphical and video resources provided.

The session on day one utilises a simple exposition strategy, with the aim of filling in any gaps in knowledge and understanding left by the pre-work.

Key messages are reinforced in the process of visits to the various head office departments and the warehouse.

The blend

Elements	Methods	Media
Before joining the company.	Games (used as a catalyst for learners to search out information about the company). Recorded video material. Reading.	Online (Internet). Online (Internet). Web pages (Internet).
On day one.	Group presentation (welcome, overview of the day, etc.). Group visits to key departments in the office and to the warehouse. Group subject metter support (Q&A).	Classroom. Accompanied by trainer. Classroom.
Ongoing support.	Performance support / referance.	Web pages (Intranet).

The rationale

The Internet is used for the pre-work, on the assumption that employees have access to PCs and an Internet connection. In exceptional cases, the material could be provided on CD-ROM. Having this material online allows for easy updating.

Face-to-face methods are utilised for day one, allowing new starters to receive a personal welcome, socialise with each other, look around head office and gain immediate answers to their questions.

The intranet is used for ongoing support so that material can be easily accessed at any time and can be readily updated.

Recipe 6: Selling skills for financial advisers

The situation

The organisation is a large insurance company with a network of several thousand financial advisers, working from small offices and their own homes. The company is aware that sales opportunities are being lost because many of the advisers are not employing best practice selling skills and wishes to bridge this gap using a training resource.

The primary learning requirement is for interpersonal skills, although some underpinning knowledge is also required.

The financial advisers come from a variety of backgrounds and have differing levels of selling skills. As mature adults, they are relatively independent learners, strongly motivated to improve their results and thereby gain higher commissions. They are essentially pragmatists, looking for any ideas that they can apply straight away.

Because of an increased priority being placed on compliance training to meet FSA requirements, the company is reluctant to take salespeople off-job for sales skills training as well. This view is endorsed by the financial advisers for whom days away mean lost sales opportunities.

All of the advisers are issued with laptops and PDAs (Personal Digital Assistants – palmtop computers). Their managers are able to join them in the field from time to time, but have too many commitments to do this regularly.

The strategy

The company has decided to adopt two strategies employing the same learning materials. For those advisers requiring a more formal introduction to selling skills, they will use structured instruction. As an ongoing resource for all advisers, they will use an exploration strategy, allowing advisers to make use of the materials as they see fit.

The blend

Elements	Methods	Media
Formal sales training.	Interactive self-study msterials (to cover the underpinning knowledge).	Online over the intranet (with option to download for offline use on PDAs).
	Recorded video material (to demonstrate sales skills in a wide variety of situations).	As above.
	One-to-one subject matter support ('ask the expert').	Email.
	Facilitated group discussion.	Bulletin board.
	On-to-one coaching.	Face-to-face (with managers).
Ongoing performance support.	As above, but accessed on an on-demand, just in time basis.	As above.

The rationale

The learning materials are organised as a library of learning objects which can be fashioned into formal courses or accessed on a random-access basis via an LCMS (Learning Content Management System). This library will be continuously updated with further video demonstrations, case histories and other resources. As all advisers have access to laptops with broadband connections, these learning objects are made available online, with the option of downloading to the PDAs for just-in-time use on the road.

The face-to-face coaching is an important ingredient, because this allows advisers to get personalised feedback based on their performance, something that would be almost impossible to achieve online.

Recipe 7: Continuous professional development

The situation

The organisation is a large professional firm employing hundreds of consultants, the majority of whom work most of the time on customer premises. The requirement is to provide continuous professional development for the consultants to ensure they are kept abreast of all the latest ideas, developments and legislation.

The consultants are highly-educated and technically-literate young professionals, with the potential to learn independently. They travel to customer premises by train, car and plane and spend many nights in hotels.

Every consultant is equipped with a laptop and an iPod.

The strategy

The firm has decided to meet the requirement using a mix of exposition and exploration strategies, which are well-suited to the dissemination of information and knowledge, where learners are not required to formally demonstrate what they have learned. They are satisfied that the audience is sufficiently independent and experienced to be able to cope with these approaches without difficulty.

The blend

Elements	Methods	Media
Delivery.	Recorded audio material (monologues and interviews). Group lectures / presentations, including Q & A. Reading (in-depth coverage of the issues raised in the above). Facilitated group discussion of topics raised above. Individual exploration / research.	Downloadable MP3 files delivered as podcasts. 'Webinars' using virtual classroom software. Web pages on intranet. Bulletin board. Using web links listed on intranet web pages.

The rationale

Media have been chosen to provide flexible access to learners on the move and working off-site. The use of podcasts makes it possible for learners to catch up on latest information while travelling and while not online. The webinars and bulletin boards allow issues to be clarified, explored and debated in greater depth. Only the webinars are 'live' and require learners to be online at a specific time, although these could also be viewed later as recordings.

Recipe 8: Leadership training

The situation

The organisation is a major charity delivering overseas aid. Their requirement is for leadership training for their middle managers at head office and working in the field. They wish their managers to achieve a balance in their leadership behaviour between the needs of the task, the needs of the individuals in the team, and the needs of the team as a whole.

The audience consists of well-educated and motivated professionals, aged from mid 20s to late 50s. All have some leadership experience and some a considerable amount.

Head office employees are based on a single site, with a fully-equipped training centre. Employees working in the field are geographically dispersed but have access to the Internet.

The strategy

The charity has decided to adopt a guided discovery strategy, because of the importance of processes, principles and attitudes to the requirement. This strategy should also work well for learners with a reasonable amount of experience of leadership.

The blend

Elements	Methods	Media
Preparation.	Questionnaire completed by student, manager, subordinates, peers (360°), to assess starting position.	Online activity.
Delivery.	Group ice-breaking activity. Group activities / exercises. Unfacilitated group discussion (for planning and reflection). Facilitated whole group discussion (to draw out general conclusions). Individual action planning activity.	Workshop. Workshop. Workshop. Workshop. N/A.

Application.	Individual work experience. Individual reflection activity.	N/A.
		Learners each maintain a learning blog (web log).
	Unfacilitated group discussion.	Learners comment on each others' blog entries.
	One-to-one coaching.	Tutors respond to lerners' learning blog entries by adding comments.
Review.	Questionnaire completed by learner, manager, subordinates, peers (360°), to assess shift in perceptions/changes in behaviour.	Online activity.
	Group progress review.	Virtual classroom.
	Facilitated group discussion.	Virtual classroom.

The rationale

A key component of the programme is a workshop, during which learners experiment with leadership behaviour and obtain feedback through the results they achieve with the group activities and from other group members. Although it is expensive for employees working in the field to attend the workshop, the charity feels there is no feasible alternative to a face-to-face setting. Learners prepare for the workshop with a 360° feedback exercise, completed online. At the end of the workshop they make plans to apply what they have learned to the work environment.

Following the workshop, learners maintain a daily learning blog, accessible by all members of the group. The blog encourages learners to reflect on and share their real-world leadership experiences. After one month, the 360° feedback exercise is repeated and the group reconvenes online for a short review workshop.

Recipe 9: Training for air traffic controllers

The situation

The organisation is an international air traffic control training school, providing comprehensive training programmes for new air traffic controllers.

The learning requirement is multi-faceted, including knowledge of concepts, processes, principles, rules and procedures; operation of technical equipment; and advanced problem-solving and decision-making skills. Learners are typically in their twenties and thirties, computer-literate, but varying somewhat in their knowledge and experience of aviation issues.

During the period of the training, learners are residential at the training centre. Once back with their employers, they have ongoing Internet access.

The strategy

The school has chosen a strategy of structured instruction, with an element of guided discovery using simulators. It believes these strategies are the most appropriate given the emphasis on imparting knowledge and cognitive skills, and the fact that many of the learners are relative novices.

The blend

Elements	Methods	Media
Background knowledge.	Interactive self-study lessons.	Online over the school's intranet (using their own bespoke materials), within a computer classroom.
	Group activities.	Classroom.
	Facilitated group discussion.	Classroom.
	Group visit (to observe air traffic controllers at work).	N/A.

Skills development.	Group instruction. Individual practice. Repeated individual practice (observed by trainer and other learners). Group progress reviews.	Classroom. Computer classroom. Dedicated simulators (within the school). Classroom.
Application (on return from school).	Observed practice on live system. Performance support / reference.	On-job. Web pages on the internet / downloadable PDF's.

The rationale

The background knowledge element is largely accomplished in the classroom, using a mix of interactive self-study lessons and group work. The self-study component is helpful because it allows students to work at their own pace, which is important when there is a great deal of technical material to be covered and the level of starting knowledge varies. This is complemented by group activities and discussion, providing opportunities to integrate, expand on and reinforce the material.

Simulators are used to allow learners to experience a wide variety of potential situations without a risk to safety. When learners return from the school they continue to develop their skills on-job with an experienced controller.

The school provides materials for ongoing reference online, so they can be accessed easily by past students wherever they are based, and so the materials can be continuously maintained and improved.

Recipe 10: Developing presentation skills

The situation

The organisation is a small training company providing coaching to those wishing to develop their presentation skills. The company is headed up by an internationally-renown expert on public speaking and communication.

The programme provided by the company includes a knowledge component (essential concepts, principles and rules) but is primarily focused on building communication skills.

Typical learners are middle and senior managers, and sales and marketing professionals. All will have had experience of presenting and all will have the capability to learn independently if required. On the whole they are cash-rich and time-poor. They are also not keen to show up any frailties in their abilities to their peers.

The strategy

The company employs a mix of exposition, guided discovery and exploration, all geared towards experienced, independent learners who want highly individualised attention.

The blend

Elements	Methods	Media
Preparation.	Individual questionnaire (to help learner clarify their personal objectives). One-to-one planning session Individual practice (the learner makes a real presentation, observed by coach).	Online activity. Telephone. Either face-to-face (coach attends a presentation given by the learner) or remote (the learner submits video of a presentation for the coach to review).

	Reading (book by the founder of the company).	Book.
	Viewing recorded video material (featuring skills demonstrations).	DVD.
Coaching.	One-to-one coaching.	Face-to-face.
	Individual assignment (learner prepares a presentation outline and submits to coach for review).	Submitted and responded to using email.
	Individual assignment (learner prepares slides and submits to coach for review).	Submitted and responded to using email.
	Individual assignment (the learner makes a real presentation, observed by coach - as above).	Either face-to-face or remote using video (as above).
	(These four steps cycle as required).	
Application.	Performance support / ongoing reinforcement.	Downloadable MP3 files (played from the PC or as podcasts).
		Web pages on Internet (including a regular blog by the founder).

The rationale

The programme utilises offline media (books and DVD) – easily accessible anytime and anywhere – to introduce background knowledge and demonstrate core skills.

Some of the coaching is face-to-face, allowing the coach to build a strong relationship with the learner and providing opportunities for some one-to-one skills practice. At other times the dialogue continues online, primarily for the learner's convenience.

When the programme has been completed, the relationship with the learner is maintained and the key concepts reinforced by regular online communications.

Recipe 11: Training for network engineers

The situation

The organisation is an IT training company providing technical courses for IT professionals around the world. The requirement is for comprehensive training for computer engineers working on large-scale corporate networks using a wide range of hardware and software configurations.

Learners must first acquire a certain amount of background knowledge about networking (concepts, processes, principles, rules, etc.). This then needs to be applied to the technical problem-solving tasks which form the most important element of their work.

Learners are typically in their 20s and 30s, bright and technically-literate. Because they have different amounts of work experience, they vary considerably in their starting level of knowledge of the subject. Their preference is to learn through hands-on experience wherever possible.

It is prohibitively expensive to equip classrooms with the wide range of networking hardware and software required for learners to have the hands-on practice they need. On the other hand, it would be too risky for learners to practise using live networks.

The strategy

The training company has chosen to employ a mix of structured instruction and guided discovery strategies, the former for background knowledge and the latter as the basis for developing the key problem-solving skills.

The blend

Elements	Methods	Media
Background knowledge.	Interactive self study lessons. One-to-one subject matter support. Individual assessment.	Online over the Internet. Email and instant messaging. Online over the internet.
Practicle work.	Individual assignments (tasks to be completed using real network hardware and software). One-to-one subject matter support One-to-one progress review.	Online over the internet using online labs (see description below). Email and instant messaging. Email and instant messaging.
Application.	Performance support / reference.	Web pages on the internet. Downloadable PDF documents.

The rationale

The company has used interactive self-study to provide the background knowledge, because this allows learners to learn at their own pace, and in their own preferred time and place. This is particularly important given the wide variability in their starting knowledge.

Practical work is provided through online labs, which allow learners to configure real network hardware and software (provided at a central location by the training company) at a distance over the Internet. This provides a more realistic experience than a simulation, but avoids the risks associated with practising with a live system.

Individual work is backed up at all stages by online tutorial support, accessible by email and instant messaging.

Recipe 12: Healthy living

The situation

The organisation is the head office of a major insurance company, employing about a thousand white-collar workers. On the initiative of the occupational health department, they have decided to conduct a programme to educate staff about the benefits of exercise and healthy eating, and to encourage them to make positive changes in their lifestyle.

A certain amount of background knowledge is required, in the form of facts, concepts, processes, rules and principles. These need to be considered in the context of learners' existing attitudes and behaviours.

The programme is voluntary, so is only likely to attract those with a degree of motivation to change. Learners will vary widely in their age, prior knowledge and learning preferences.

Given that all participants are based at the same site, there are few practical constraints, other than that the programme should be conducted outside normal office hours.

The strategy

The programme uses a certain amount of structured instruction to provide learners with the background knowledge and understanding that they require. However, to encourage lasting changes to attitudes and behaviour, the more learner-centred strategies of guided discovery and exploration are employed as the programme progresses.

The blend

Elements	Methods	Media
Preparation.	Questionnaire. Short presentation and Q&A. Group discussion (review of questionnaire results).	Paper-based. Class. Class.
Delivery.	Interactive self study lessons.	CD-ROM (for use at home or at work).
Application.	Individual assignments (diets, exercise regimes, etc,). Group activities (hikes, runs, etc.). Individual reflection activity. Unfacilitated group discussion. Weekly group progress reviews and discussions. Ongoing reference (including links to web resources).	N/A. N/A. Students each maintain a learning blog (web log). Students comment on each others's blog entries. Class. Web pages on intranet.

The rationale

The programme includes an important face-to-face ingredient, which provides an opportunity for free discussion, and allows the group to bond and provide mutual support. The fact that these sessions take place every week is also important in keeping up peer pressure and providing encouragement.

The self-study element provides those learners who need structure with a step-by-step route to acquiring the necessary knowledge and understanding. This material would need to be engaging, highly interactive and encourage reflection. More independent learners could explore the online reference materials and web links.

The requirement for learners to complete a learning blog maintains the programme's momentum throughout the week, encouraging openness and collaboration.

Recipe 13: Language learning

The situation

The organisation is a manufacturer of defence equipment which has recently agreed a major, long-term partnership deal with a French firm, which will involve them working closely together on a number of new development projects. To encourage a close and friendly relationship with their partner, the company is initiating a three month-long campaign to improve the French-language skills of around 100 employees who will be assigned to the projects from the beginning.

Learners will be expected to achieve only a basic level of capability with written and spoken French, as English will be the business language and French-fluent personnel will be assigned to posts requiring close liaison.

The target audience consists primarily of engineers, well-educated but with only basic school French, working at one major site. They will be allowed a certain amount of time off each week to complete the programme, but could not be released for intensive, face-to-face courses.

The strategy

The programme employs a structured instruction strategy, which is well suited to the systematic teaching of vocabulary, grammar and communication skills.

The blend

Elements	Methods	Media
Preparation.	One-to-one pre-assessment.	Face-to-face.
Delivery.	Interactive self-study lessons (with audio and video). Weekly, 90-minute sessions including group instruction and practicle conversational exercises. Individual written assignments.	CD-ROM (for use at home or work). Class.
	Individual and group assignments, including periods of communicating with each other only in French, whether face-to-face, by email or on the telephone.	Submitted by email to tutor for assessment. N/A.

The rationale

The programme requires a face-to-face component, so learners can practise their conversational French and receive feedback. These activities could also be undertaken in a virtual classroom, but this facility is not needed because learners are all based on the same site.

The self-study component allows learners to acquire basic vocabulary and grammar at their own pace, and at a time and place that suits them. The self-study component will be individually tailored depending on learners' performance in the initial one-to-one assessments.

The programme also makes use of the real working environment to provide opportunities for ongoing practice.

Recipe 14: Diversity training

The situation

The organisation is a telecommunications company employing around 2000 white collar and blue collar staff. As part of a broad management initiative to encourage a more diverse and harmonious workforce, and to avoid claims arising because of infringements to equal opportunities legislation, the company intends to have all employees participate in a diversity training programme. There is a small knowledge component to the training, but the main requirement is to shift attitudes positively towards diversity both as a concept and in terms of actual behaviour.

Learners vary dramatically in terms of age, educational level, the type of work they do and their existing attitudes to diversity. Most are technically literate and all have access to computers, whether at their desk, in dedicated learning centres or at home.

The strategy

The company has chosen to adopt a guided discovery approach to the training, as they feel this provides the best chance to positively influence attitudes.

The blend

Elements	Methods	Media
Preparation.	Confidential questionnaire re attitudes to diversity (pre course). One-hour interactive self-study programme, including stories, personal accounts and case studies.	Online on the intranet. CD-ROM (for use at home or work).
Delivery.	Group ice-breaking activity. Group activity including games and role plays. Facilitated group discussion.	Class. Class. Class.

Application.	Reading (case studies, updates to legislation, etc.). Facilitated group discussion.	Web pages on intranet. Bulletin board.
Evaluation.	Confidential questionnaire re attitudes to diversity (post course).	Online on the intranet.

The rationale

The centrepiece of the course is a face-to-face workshop in which learners participate in a series of activities designed to provide new perspectives on diversity. These activities need to be conducted in a social context in which learners find it easy to reflect and share their thoughts and experiences, making the classroom the obvious choice.

The introductory CD-ROM allows learners to acquire a basic knowledge of diversity concepts and current legislation in their own time. It also raises a number of issues for learners to reflect on in advance of the workshop.

The intranet provides a means to keep the messages from the course alive and to encourage ongoing debate using a bulletin board.

Recipe 15: Basic literacy

The situation

The organisation is a training provider specialising in adult numeracy and literacy. They have a contract to provide basic literacy training to employees of a major car manufacturer wishing to develop their skills in order to improve their career prospects.

The learning is essentially knowledge-based, comprising facts, concepts, rules and principles.

Typical learners are poorly educated and likely to have had unhappy experiences of learning in the past. They have access to computers and meeting room facilities in the company's open learning centre.

The strategy

The training provider uses structured instruction to meet the requirement, which is well suited to the nature of the subject and provides the structure that these learners are likely to require.

The blend

Elements	Methods	Media
Preparation.	One-to-one review.	Face-to-face.
Delivery.	Interactive self-study lessons. Individual drill and practice. Written assignments.	Online web-based delivery. Online web-based delivery. Submitted as email attachements; feedback by email.
	One-to-one coaching (one hour per fortnight).	Face-to-face.
Application.	Ongoing reference. One-to-one subject matter support.	Web pages on the intrrenet Email.

The rationale

Although the coaching relationship could have been conducted entirely online, the provider has chosen to mix in a regular face-to-face element, to provide additional structure and personal support to learners who are unlikely to want to work entirely independently.

Otherwise, the key literacy concepts are delivered using interactive lessons and drill and practice exercises, accessed online. These allow learners to work at their own pace and obtain the amount of intensive practice required if they are to significantly improve their skills.

The written assignments are submitted and reviewed online, reducing the need for face-to-face contact time.

Recipe 16: Handling customer complaints

The situation

The organisation is a large multinational telecommunications company based in London. The organisation has realised that customer service is a key differentiator in its market and that if they can provide higher levels of service then this will help them to retain customers and to win new business. The organisation is also finding that the process of dealing with complaints is putting an enormous amount of stress on employees.

The learning requirement is multi-faceted: instilling the motivation to ensure that complaints are dealt with efficiently, developing the soft skills to handle customers sensitively, and providing knowledge of the processes and procedures that need to be followed.

Because of the high volume of sales that the organisation is currently managing, approximately 1500 employees need to be trained in complaint handling.

The strategy

The organisation has chosen to use a structured instruction strategy, applied using a wide variety of learning media in a blended approach.

The blend

Elements	Methods	Media
Preparation.	Collecting examples of good and bad customer service.	Email / paper / anecdotes.
Motivation.	Viewing recorded video material (demonstrating the cost of losing a customer). Facilitated group discussion about the importance of handling complaints effectively.	DVDs in the classroom. Classroom.

Soft skills.	Individual practice using role play exercises.	Classroom.
Processes and procedures.	Interactive self-study materials, providing proof of learning. Scenario based, asking learners how they would respond to a situation and then providing feedback. Performance support / reference.	Online over the intranet. Paper-based job aids.
Ongoing support.	Coaching to help learners maintain their motivation and their customer handling skills.	Group surgeries. One-to-one support.

The rationale

An important objective of this training is to maintain high levels of motivation in the workplace and the organisation felt that this would be best accomplished using video and discussion in a classroom setting.

It is important for regulatory reasons that employees follow a specific complaint handling procedure and this was trained most efficiently using a one hour e-learning module, backed up by job aids. The e-learning provides proof of learning, which is important as this training is a key element of a strategy designed to retain and win back customers.

Recipe 17: Electronic records management system

The situation

The organisation is a large government department located across multiple sites in the UK. In response to e-Government initiatives, a new Electronic Records Management System (ERM) is being installed.

About 5000 employees need to know about the new system and its related processes and procedures, but the key to success is winning over hearts and minds and convincing staff that change is not only necessary but beneficial. The department believes there could be a great deal of resistance to the change and that they therefore need to take a 'hand holding' approach.

An important secondary objective is the department's desire to pilot e-learning.

As this is a high profile project, it requires a substantial internal marketing effort over a sustained period.

The strategy

The department has chosen to adopt a mix of learning strategies, including guided discovery in the process of building motivation, structured instruction for teaching the processes and procedures, and an element of exploration in the wide variety of follow-up methods.

The blend

Elements	Methods	Media
Motivation.	Group presentations in the form of road shows to explain the planned changes, delivered by senior civil servants six months prior to the training.	Face-to-face events

	Group presentation and discussion in the form of structured meetings with their manager, designed to reinforce the road shows and provide a channel to address concerns.	Face-to-face meetings
Marketing.	Reading material provided through a website available six months before the launch and providing an identity for the project.	Online over the intranet
	A series of pioneering pilot projects across the Department. Each is high profile, given high visibility and used to positively promote the change.	N/A
Processes and procedures.	Workshops designed to provide a high level overview of the new system, including hands-on practical sessions.	Classroom
	Scenario-based, interactive self-study materials.	A Learning Zone with allocated slots for each employee. Twenty employees at a time complete a two hour e-learning course with floorwalkers available for support.
Follow up.	Opportunity to refresh the self-study training.	Learning Café allowing employees to drop in for a refresher of the training and ask questions in a relaxed environment
	Performance support / reference in the form of a desktop-based, step-by-step guide, providing show-me, try-me functionality.	Online over the intranet
	One-to-one support.	Provided face-to-face, using floor walkers and product champions across the Department.

The rationale

The department has chosen an approach that leverages the scale efficiencies provided by e-learning but maintains the human touch provided by classroom training. They have also ensured that on-going support is always available via a number of dedicated channels.

This is a big change for the department but it is vital that the new systems and processes are embedded quickly. Reverting back to the paper-based system after launch is not an option. The history of poorly run Government IT programmes is on the implementation team's mind. They have decided to take an approach that makes multiple interventions available, catering for different learning styles. From the start the approach has been designed to keep people informed; to drive change from within.

Recipe 18: Compliance training

The situation

The organisation is a large utility with a mobile workforce which rarely visits an office. The organisation needs to prove that they are compliant with health and safety procedures on an ongoing basis. Compliance with this requirement is open to external scrutiny, so non-compliance risks damage to the organisation's reputation and the possibility of fines.

The organisation feels that neither classroom training nor e-learning are practical options, given the geographic spread of the workforce and patchy access to PCs.

The strategy

The organisation has adopted a simple structured instruction strategy, applied using an innovative combination of learning media.

The blend

Elements	Methods	Media
Processes and procedures.	Recorded audio, including scenarios designed to make employees think about how they would handle particular situations and to provide important information. Self-study materials to capture answers and provide further information.	Audio CD Workbooks (employees were asked to bring these with them to the subsequent meeting with their manager for review)
Motivation.	Management briefings, used to provide high-level information and check understanding.	Face-to-face sessions

Testing for compliance.	Individual assessment.	A telephone-based assessment with a set of randomly-selected questions. Employees call in from any telephone, key in their unique identification and complete the proof of learning. Results are stored in a web-based database.

The rationale

It is important that the company can prove compliance and that it can renew employee accreditation, quickly and efficiently. The combination of audio CD and workbook provides a simple way to provide engaging self-study learning. The telephone-based assessment provides an innovative, automated way to check and record understanding, without the need for computers. Importantly, the management sessions provide support and a channel for issues and concerns to be resolved.

Appendix 1: Responding to the situation

This table examines the implications of particular situational variables when making your choice from the four main training strategies described by Clark and Whittrock (2001)[1] and when choosing the learning medium. Where several alternative strategies are listed, the author's preference is listed first. In practice, choice of strategy is also likely to be influenced by the training and learning culture in your organisation. For more information on the four training strategies, see Appendix 2.

Situational variable	Suggested training strategy	Implications for selection of learning medium
Nature of the learning		
Knowledge of facts and concepts.	Structured instruction. Exposition (with care to avoid overload). Exploration (where there is not a need to demonstrate particular learning).	A self-paced element may be advantageous.
Knowledge and understanding of processes and principles.	Guided discovery (e.g. simulations, games, case studies, projects, assignments, discussion, coaching). Structures instruction. Exposition (with care to avoid overload). Exploration (where there is not a need to demonstrate particular learning).	A self-paced element may be advantageous.
Knowledge and understanding of rules and procedures.	Structured instruction. Exposition (with care to avoid overload). Exploration (where there is not a need to demonstrate particular learning).	A self-paced element may be advantageous.
Cognitive (problem-solving) skills.	Structured instruction (e.g. drill and practice). Guided discovery (e.g. simulations, games, case studies, projects, assignments, discussion, coaching).	

Social (interpersonal) skills.	Structured instruction (e.g. role plays).	The training will normally require a face-to-face element to allow for realistic practice of the skills.
Psychomotor (physical) skills.	Structured instruction (one-to-one or group).	Training will typically need to be face-to-face.
Attitudinal change.	Exposition (e.g.stories, personal accounts). Guided discovery (e.g. questionnaires case studies, simulations, role play, group discussion).	
Learner Characteristics		
Learner is capable of learning independently.	Learner will be comfortable with any of the strategies, but is likely to prefer exploration.	
Learner is dependent on trainer for structure.	Will learn best with structured instruction or guided discovery.	
Learner is a novice in the subject being taught.	Will learn best with structured instruction or guided discovery.	
Learner experienced in subject being taught.	Learner will be comfortable with any of the strategies.	
Learner is an activist.	Likely to prefer guided discovery, the practicle elements of structured instruction, and exploration (becasue they control the pace).	
Learner is a theorist.	Any of the strategies can have a theoretical component, but most likely to prefer exposition and structured instruction.	
Learner is a reflector.	Likely to prefer guided discovery and exploration, particulary the oppertunities for discussion.	

Learner is a pragmatist	Will prefer whichever strategy will deliver relevant, usuable knowledge and skills the quickest.	
Practicle Contraints		
Learners are widely dispersed geographically		Classroom training will be more time-consuming and expensive. If time zones vary widely, will make it more difficult to rganise real-time online events.
Learners find it hard to allocate large blocks of time during the working day.		Classroom training will be more difficult to schedule.
There is only a small audience for the training.		Favours media that requires less design and development.
Time available to complete the training is limited.		Favours media that requires less design and development. Favours media that delivers the required learning in the shortest time (typically modular and self-paced).
Access to computers is limited.		Makes any computer-based delivery harder to accommodate.
Access to suitable computer network connections are limited.		Makes online delivery more difficult.
Access to traiing facilities are limited.		Assuing outside facilities cannot be rented, classroom training will be more difficult to accomodate.
Trainer time is limited.		Assuming outsourcing is not an option, the situation favours self-study media.

Appendix 2: Training strategies and supporting methods

This table provides examples of training methods likely to be supportive of each of the four main training strategies described by Clark and Whittrock (2001)[2]. Typically a selection of these methods will be required to fulfil the strategy. Note that different strategies could be employed at different stages in a learning intervention. See Appendix 3 for examples of media options applicable to each training method.

Strategy	Supporting Training Methods
Exposition (training by telling). *Learning model: Learner as a sponge or spectator; absorbs information provided.*	Prescribed reading. Viewing recorded video material. Listening to recorded audio material. Viewing slide presentations with recorded narration. Group lecture / presentation. Subject matter support (Q&A). Individual test / assessment Performance support / reference.
Structured instruction. *Learning model: Learner as a builder of associations through responses to carefully planned stimuli.*	Interactive self-study lesson / tutorial. Group or one-to-one instruction. Subject matter support (Q&A). Facilitated group discussion. Individual drill and practice. Individual practice (observed by trainer and/or other learners). Individual test / assessment. Group or one-to-one progress review. Performance support / reference.
Guided discovery. *Learning model: Learner as a problem solver.*	Group ice-breaking activity. Questionnaire / inventory. Individual or group planning activity. Individual or group activity / exercise (e.g. a case study, problem-solving task, scenario). Individual or group game or simulation. Individual or group project or assignment. Individual or group visit. Individual or group reflection activity. Individual work experience. Facilitated group discussion. One-to-one coaching or mentoring. Group or one-to-one progress review.

Exploration. *Learning model: Learner as a active builder of knowledge.*	Individual exploration/research. Reading. Viewing recorded video material. Listening to recorded audio material. Viewing slide presentations with recorded narration. Questionnaire / inventory. Performance support / reference. Subject matter support (Q&A). Unfacilitated group discussion (e.g. using a bulletin board / blogs). Attendance at lectures / presentations.

Appendix 3: Training methods and options for their delivery

This table lists a selection of training methods and provides examples of media that could be used for their delivery. Do not be constrained by this list as you will no doubt be able to come with additional methods and further ways in which the methods listed here can be realised. For an analysis of the comparative benefits of the various media options, see Appendix 4.

Method	Media Options
Individual	
Reading.	Books / other printed materials Workbook. Documents contained on removable computer media (CD-ROMs, etc.). The web (Internet or intranet). Downloadable documents (PDF, Word, PowerPoint, etc.).
Viewing recorded video material.	Downloadable video files for playback on computers and personal media players ('vodcasts'). Playback on computer from removable computer media (CD-ROMs, etc.). Streamed delivery from the Internet or intranet. Playback during a virtual classroom session. Playback on VCRs, DVD players, etc. using removable media. Broadcast transmission (TV). Playback during face-to-face events.
Listening to recorded audio material.	Downloadable video files for playback on computers and personal media players ('vodcasts'). Playback on computer from removable computer media (CD-ROMs, etc.). Streamed delivery from the Internet or intranet. Playback during a virtual classroom session. Playback on VCRs, DVD players, etc. using removable media. Broadcast transmission (TV). Playback during face-to-face events.

Individual planning activity.	Unsupported activity (requires no media) Exercise in workbook Exercise on CD-ROM / other removable media Exercise online (Internet or intranet)
Individual reflection activity.	Unsupported activity (requires no media) Exercise in workbook Exercise on CD-ROM / other removable media Exercise online (Internet or intranet) Maintaining a web log ('blog')
Individual exploration/research.	Unsupported activity (requires no media). Resources could include all media listed above under 'prescribed reading', 'viewing recorded video material' and 'listening to recorded audio material' Attendance at seminars or conferences
Questionnaire / survey / inventory (including 360° feedback methods).	Paper-based activity. Online activity (Internet or intranet).
Interactive self-study lesson / tutorial.	In workbook. On CD-ROM / other removable media. Online web-based delivery (Internet or intranet).
Individual activity or exercise (e.g. a case study, problem-solving task, scenario).	On CD-ROM / other removable media. Online web-based delivery (Internet or intranet).
Individual game or simulation.	On CD-ROM / other removable media. Online web-based delivery (Internet or intranet). Use of dedicated simulator.
Individual drill and practice.	Exercise in workbook. On CD-ROM / other removable media. Online delivery (Internet or intranet).
Individual test / assessment.	Exercise in workbook. On CD-ROM / other removable media. Online delivery (Internet or intranet).
Individual assignment / project.	Unsupported activity (requires no media). The assignment could be set up and followed up using a wide variety of media.
Individual visit (to observe the work of others / to share experiences).	Face-to-face. The visit could be set up using a wide variety of media.

Individual work experience.	Unsupported activity (requires no media).
Performance support / reference.	Books / other printed materials. On CD-ROM / other removable media. The web (Internet or intranet). Downloadable documents (PDF, Word, PowerPoint, etc.).
One-to-one	
One-to-one instruction.	Face-to-face (on-job or off-job). Virtual classroom (possible but unusual).
One-to-one subject matter support (Q&A).	Face-to-face. Email / SMS messaging. Instant messaging. Telephone.
One-to-one coaching or mentoring.	Face-to-face. Email / SMS messaging. Instant messaging. Telephone.
One-to-one progress review.	Face-to-face. Email / SMS messaging. Instant messaging. Telephone.
Group	
Group ice-breaking activity.	Workshop/class. Bulletin board. Virtual classroom. Text-based chat. Teleconference.
Group energising activity.	Workshop/class. Virtual classroom. Text-based chat.
Group lecture / presentation.	Seminar/conference. Workshop/class. Virtual classroom / 'webinar'. [Note that recorded lectures can be distributed for individual. listening/viewing using a wide variety of online and offline. media. Presentations can be distributed as narrated. PowerPoint shows for individual access online.].

Group instruction.	Workshop/class. Small group (on-job). Virtual classroom.
Group subject matter support (Q&A).	Workshop/class. Bulletin board. Virtual classroom. Text-based chat. Teleconference.
Facilitated group discussion.	Workshop/class. Bulletin board. Virtual classroom. Text-based chat. Teleconference
Unfacilitated group discussion (e.g. for planning, reflection).	Workshop/class (as a syndicate). Bulletin board. Virtual classroom. Text-based chat. Teleconference. Web logs (blogs).
Group activity / exercise (e.g. a case study, problem-solving task, scenario).	Workshop/class. Bulletin board. Virtual classroom.
Multi-player or group game or simulation.	Workshop/class. Virtual classroom. Online web-based delivery (Internet or intranet). Use of dedicated simulator(s).
Individual practice (observed by trainer and/or other learners).	Workshop/class. Small group (on-job). Virtual classroom (possible but unusual).
Group project or assignment.	Unsupported activity (requires no media). The assignment could be set up using a wide variety of media. Ongoing group collaboration could be supported by email/SMS messaging, instant messaging, text-based chat, bulletin boards, wikis (web sites that are easily editable by users), the telephone and face-to-face meetings.

Group visit (to observe the work of others / to share experiences).	Face-to-face. The visit could be set up using a wide variety of media.
Group progress review.	Workshop/class. Small group (on-job). Bulletin board. Virtual classroom. Text-based chat. Teleconference.

Appendix 4: Comparative benefits of learning media

This table lists the principal practical and learning benefits of the most common learning media. It can be used as a reference when selecting the most appropriate medium for the delivery of a chosen learning method. For a list of learning methods and the options available for their delivery, see Appendix 3.

	Practical benefits	Learning benefits
Offline media		
Books / other printed materials.	Portable, easy-to-use.	Potential for very high resolution text and still images.
Workbook.	Portable, easy-to-use.	Encourages limited interactivity when used for self-study.. Can include still images.
Video (cassette, DVD) / also broadcast TV.	Can be watched at home or in a training room without the need for a PC.	Potential for high quality video and audio.
Audio (cassette, CD) / also broadcast radio.	Can be listened to at home or in a training room without the need for a PC. Can be listened to in cars or using portable music players while on the move.	Potential for high quality audio.
Removable computer media (CD-ROM/DVD-ROM/Flash cards, etc.)	Usable on any computer or mobile device with the appropriate drive, whether or not there is a network connection. No bandwidth constraints. Much cheaper to replicate and less bulky than printed materials.	Can contain a wide variety of digital media including text, still images, animation, audio, video, PDF files and Office documents. Can contain all forms of interactive, self-study materials, including assessments, tutorials, games and simulations.

Simulator.	Allows students to develop complex skills without the need for access to the real equipment or job environment and without risk to safety.	Students can experiment with manoeuvres that would be too risky or expensive using real equipment in the real job environment.
Online media. (via PCs, mobile devices, digital TV).	All online media benefit from the capability for remote access, eliminating the time and cost incurred in travel for students and tutors.	
The web (Internet or intranet).	An unlimited amount of information can be made available extremely cheaply. Information can be accessed from any location where a network connection is available Audio and video can be streamed to the user, obviating the need for download. Students can control when they access material and for how long Information on student activity and progress can be automatically stored centrally. Because the information is maintained centrally, the student sees only the latest material.	Can contain a wide variety of digital media including text, still images, animation, audio and video. Can contain all forms of interactive, self-study materials, including assessments, tutorials, games and simulations. Provides the (rarely used) capability for multi-player games and simulations.
Downloadable documents (PDF, Word, PowerPoint, etc.).	An unlimited number of documents can be made available extremely cheaply. Documents can be accessed from any location where a network connection is available.	Depending on their type, documents can contain a wide variety of digital media formats.
Downloadable media files (audio, video, Flash movies).	An unlimited number of media files can be made available extremely cheaply. The media files can be downloaded wherever a network connection is available. Can be copied to portable media players for access while on the move (podcasts, etc.).	Potential for high quality video and audio. Flash movies can support all forms of interactive self-study, including assessments, tutorials, games and simulations.

Email / desktop alerts / SMS messaging.	Because communication is asynchronous, the student is not tied to a specific timetable.	Provides a student with asynchronous access to tutors and other learners.
Instant messaging.	Can achieve a quicker response than email. Informs the user when their contacts are online. VOIP (voice over the Internet) provides an alternative to the telephone, without call charges.	Provides a student with real-time access to tutors and other learners, with the option of audio and video communication.
Text-based chat.	Easy to implement and to use.	Provides a student with the opportunity for real-time collaboration with other learners.
Bulletin board / forum.	Because communication is asynchronous, the student is not tied to a specific timetable.	Provides a student with the opportunity for asynchronous collaboration with other learners. Benefits those students who do not enjoy real-time group collaboration.
Web log ('blog').	Because communication is asynchronous, the student is not tied to a specific timetable.	Encourages reflection. Provides a student with the opportunity for asynchronous collaboration, by adding comments to other learners' blogs and by responding to comments made on their own blogs. Benefits those students who do not enjoy real-time group collaboration.
Virtual classroom / web conferencing.	Virtual classroom sessions can be recorded for those who miss the live session. Experts do not have to travel in order to participate, making it easier to call on experts from anywhere in the world.	Provides an online alternative to the classroom for real-time one-to-one, small group and large group communication and collaboration. Includes the capacity for real-time audio and video-based communication. Allows for application sharing which can be useful for IT training.

Telephone.		
Automated, individual access.	Simple and universally-available.	Provides access to recorded audio information and to assessments using audio-based questions.
One-to-one call.	Simple and familiar technology, with which most students will be comfortable.	Allows real-time voice communication between a student and their tutor.
Teleconference.	As above, although requires more planning than a simple one-to-one call.	Allows real-time voice communication between groups of students and their tutor.
Face-to-face.	In most cases, face-to-face events are relatively free from interruptions and allow students to block-book their learning time.	Face-to-face communication in general is real-time, multi-sensory and highly flexible.
One-to-one interaction.	Interaction can take place in the work environment (on-job).	Provides a high degree of personalisation. Students can observe real-world behaviour and practise in an authentic setting.
Facilitated, on-job small group interaction.	Interaction can take place in the work environment (on-job). More efficient in terms of trainer time than one-to-one interaction.	Students can observe real-world behaviour and practise in an authentic setting. Provides students with the opportunity for real-time collaboration.
Unfacilitated small group interaction (outside the classroom).	Groups of students can meet without travelling to a central location.	Provides students with the opportunity for real-time collaboration.
Workshop/class.	A highly-flexible and familiar format that is relatively easy to administer.	Supports a very wide variety of learning methods. The trainer can augment their delivery with flip chart, whiteboards, slides, videos, models, etc.

		Participants can work in small groups where required. Equipment (machines, etc.) can be brought into the classroom to allow demonstrations and practise. When computers are provided for all participants, students can practise computer-based skills.
Seminar / conference.	Allows large numbers of students to be addressed simultaneously, thus reducing trainer cost-per-student.	The trainer can augment their delivery with slides, videos, etc. Allows for limited trainer-student interaction.
Unsupported individual activities requiring no media.	Just to emphasise that not all learning activities need to be mediated.	Every day that we are at work is a learning opportunity!

About the author

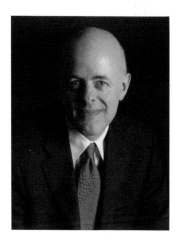

Clive Shepherd MA FCIPD FIIT MCMI

Clive Shepherd is a consultant specialising in the application of technology to education, training and employee communications. With more than twenty years of experience in this field, Clive is acknowledged as a thought leader in all aspects of e-learning and blended learning.

Clive developed his interest in interactive media at American Express in the early eighties, where he was Director of Training and Creative Services. He was also a co-founder of Epic Group plc, a leading content developer.

Since 1997, Clive has worked with a wide range of public and private sector organisations on the application of technology to learning and employee communications. For the Institute of IT Training, Clive developed an accreditation programme for e-learning providers, quality standards for e-learning materials and a competency framework for e-learning professionals. This framework formed the basis for the Certified e-Learning Professional Programme, which Clive designed with the Training Foundation, for whom he is e-Learning Director. Clive is also a founding Director of Above and Beyond Ltd, a Brighton-based content developer and publisher.

In 2003 he received the Colin Corder Award for services to IT training, and in 2004 the award for Outstanding Contribution to the Training Industry at the World of Learning conference. Clive's writing on e-learning can be found in his three previous books and more than 100 published articles. He has a monthly column in IT Training and Learning & Development magazines and posts regularly to his blog, Clive on Learning. He is also a regular speaker at UK and international conferences.

He lives in Brighton with his wife Susan. When he gets away from all things e-learning he likes to walk on the South Downs, play tennis and keep fit generally. He's also a keen musician.

Tel: +44 (0)1273561714
Blog: http://clive-shepherd.blogspot.com

If you want to find out more about Blended Learning please contact Saffron
Interactive on info@saffroninteractive.com

SAFFRON
INTERACTIVE

Northburgh House
10 Northburgh Street
London
EC1V 0AT

Tel: 0207 490 9930
Fax: 0207 253 5248
info@saffroninteractive.com
www.saffroninteractive.com